378279

I love reading

Fun at the Farm

by Ruth Owen

Editorial consultant: Mitch Cronick

D0264589

CONTENTS

Words in **bold** are explained in the glossary.

Fun at the farm

Today we are going to a **farm**!

Look at the tractor

The tractor does lots of work on the farm.

Time to cut the wheat

The **combine harvester** cuts the **wheat**.

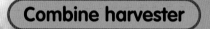

Combine harvester

Wheat

8

Wheat is made into flour.
Flour is made into bread.

Wheat

Flour

Bread

Look at the lambs

The mother sheep has two lambs.

Lamb

Lambs drink milk from their mum's udder.

Udder

Meet Ben

Ben is a sheepdog.

Ben makes the sheep go into the pen.

13

Let's look for eggs

Chickens lay eggs.

We can collect them.

Meet the pigs

The mother pig has seven piglets.

Piglet

Look at the calf

The calf drinks milk from his mum.

Calf

Milk

We drink milk too!

FALKIRK COUNCIL
LIBRARY SUPPORT
FOR SCHOOLS

One cow makes 100 glasses
of milk every day!

21

Glossary

combine harvester
A big machine that cuts down wheat and other plants. It separates the wheat grains from the stalks.

farm

A place where food is produced. Wheat, vegetables and fruit grow on farms. We get eggs, milk and meat from farms, too.

wheat

A plant that can be made into flour. The flour is used to make bread, biscuits and cakes.

23

Index

An Hachette UK Company
www.hachette.co.uk
Copyright © Octopus Publishing Group Ltd 2013
First published in Great Britain in 2010 by TickTock, an imprint of Octopus Publishing Group Ltd,
Endeavour House, 189 Shaftesbury Avenue, London WC2H 8JY.
www.octopusbooks.co.uk

ISBN 978 1 84898 232 1

Printed in China
1 3 5 7 9 10 8 6 4 2

All rights reserved. No part of this work may be reproduced or utilised in any form or by any means, electronic or
mechanical, including photocopying, recording or by any information storage and retrieval system,
without the prior written permission of the publisher.

Picture credits (t=top, b=bottom, c=centre, l=left, r=right, OFC= outside front cover, OBC=outside back cover):
iStock: 5 (man), 7 (both), 9c, 20–21. Shutterstock: OFC, Flap, 1, 2, 4–5, 6 (both), 8, 9t, 9b, 10, 11, 12,
13, 14–15, 15t, 16–17, 18–19, 22, 23, OBC.

A CIP catalogue record for this book is available from the British Library. All rights reserved. No part of this publication
may be reproduced, copied, stored in a retrieval system or transmitted in any form or by any means electronic,
mechanical, photocopying, recording or otherwise without prior written permission of the copyright owner.

24